Nathaniel Talking

Nathaniel Talking

Text copyright © 1988 by Eloise Greenfield
Illustrations © 1988 by Jan Spivey Gilchrist
Designed by Cheryl Hanna
All rights reserved.

Library of Congress Cataloging Card Number 88-51011
ISBN: 0 86316 200 2 cloth   0 86316 201 0 paper
Illustrations reproduced in Duo-Tone

Published by *Writers and Readers Publishing, Inc.*
for *Black Butterfly Children's Books*

Manufactured in Hong Kong

"Nathaniel's Rap" published in Ebony Jr. April 1982
"Grandma's Bones" published in Ebony Jr.
August/September 1984
"Making Friends" published in Ebony Jr. January 1985
"My Daddy" published in Ebony Jr. June 1985

Acknowledgement:

My thanks to great musician Brother Ah
(Robert Northern) for sharing his knowledge of the
history of bones. I am grateful also to the National
Endowment for the Arts in Washington, D.C., a Federal
Agency, and the D.C. Commission on the Arts and
Humanities for their generous support of my work.
EG

The epigraph is taken from *Black Child* by Tom Feelings
and Joyce Carol Thomas, text copyright © 1981 by
Joyce Carol Thomas, published by Zamani Productions.

Nathaniel Talking

by Eloise Greenfield

illustrated by Jan Spivey Gilchrist

Black Butterfly Children's Books
New York

To the memory of
Geraldine L. Wilson
African American poet and scholar
who let so much of her glorious light
shine on children
E G

To Michael,
William Kelvin
and children everywhere
J S G

Epigraph:

I am hewn from
    the solid ledge of rock
    the soaring songs of birds
    the rocking motions of the ocean
    the uplifted branches of the tree

I am a root
    that will be free

Joyce Carol Thomas
BLACK CHILD

Nathaniel's Rap

It's Nathaniel talking
and Nathaniel's me
I'm talking about
My philosophy
About the things I do
And the people I see
All told in the words
Of Nathaniel B. Free
That's me
And I can rap
I can rap
I can rap, rap, rap
Till your earflaps flap
I can talk that talk
Till you go for a walk
I can run it on down
Till you get out of town
I can rap

I can rap
Rested, dressed and feeling fine
I've got something on my mind
Friends and kin and neighborhood
Listen now and listen good
Nathaniel's talking
Nathaniel B. Free
Talking about
My philosophy
Been thinking all day
I got a lot to say
Gotta run it on down
Nathaniel's way
Okay!
I gotta rap
Gotta rap
Gotta rap, rap, rap
Till your earflaps flap

Gotta talk that talk
Till you go for a walk
Gotta run it on down
Till you get out of town
Gotta rap
Gotta rap
Rested, dressed and feeling fine
I've got something on my mind
Friends and kin and neighborhood
Listen now and listen good
I'm gonna rap, hey!
Gonna rap, hey!
Gonna rap, hey!
I'm gonna rap!

Nine

Nine is fine
Without a doubt
A wonderful age to be
I know that's what I thought
About eight, seven, six,
Five and four
(Did I think it, too, about three?)
But nine is really fine

Me and these friends of mine
Walk all over the neighborhood
Yes, our parents said we could
We're not babies anymore
We're old enough to know the score
We don't toe that same old line
Now that we're nine

Knowledge

I've got it all figured out
by the time I'm an old man
I'm going to know almost
everything about everything
but I'll bet on my ninety-fifth
birthday
some little girl will

come up to me and say
Mr. Nathaniel why doesn't
the such-and-such do
so-and-so
and I'll have to say
I don't know

Missing Mama

last year when Mama died
I went to my room to hide
from the hurt
I closed my door
wasn't going to come out
no more, never
but my uncle he said

you going to get past
this pain
        you going to
push on past this pain
and one of these days
you going to feel like
yourself again

I don't miss a day
remembering Mama
sometimes I cry
but mostly
I think about
the good things
now

Mama

Mama was funny
was full of jokes
was pretty
dark brown-skinned
laughter
was hard hugs
and kisses
a mad mama
sometimes
but always
always
was love

Making Friends

when I was in kindergarten
this new girl came in our class one day
and the teacher told her to sit beside me
and I didn't know what to say
so I wiggled my nose and made my bunny face

and she laughed
then she puffed out her cheeks
and she made a funny face
and I laughed
so then
we were friends

When I Misbehave

when I misbehave and have to
stay after school
my teacher don't like it
my grandma don't like it
my daddy don't like it
and when they get to talking
neither do I
I'm ready to cry

Education

one day I was dumb enough
to let somebody bet me
into a fight
and then I was mad with two
stupid boys
the one who was hitting me
and the one who was hitting
him

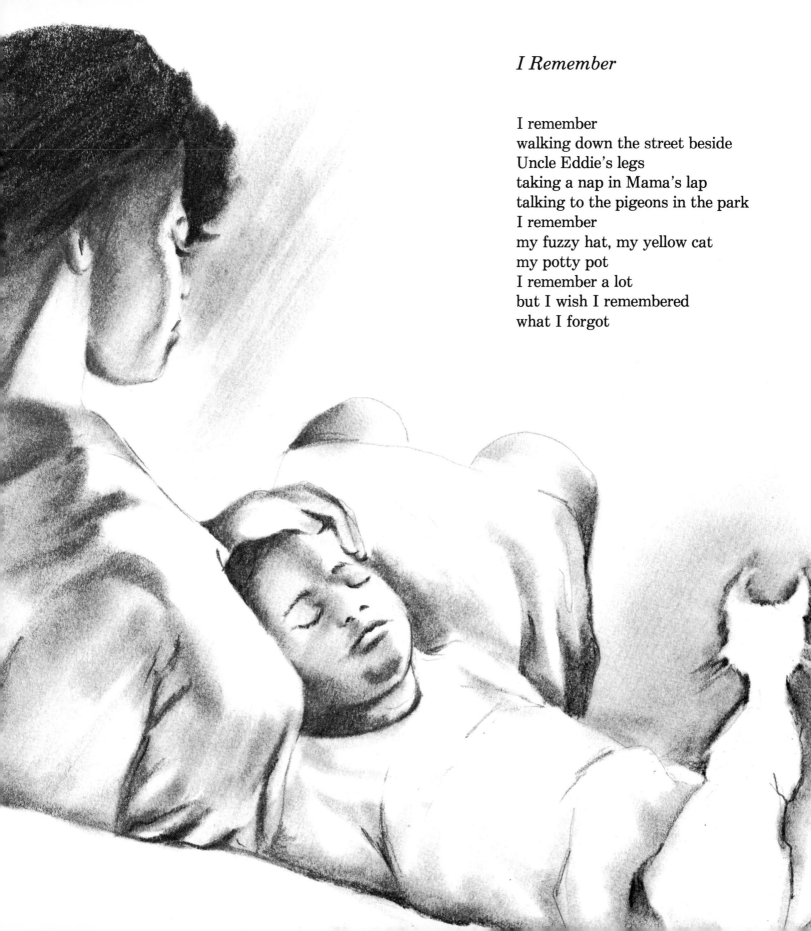

I Remember

I remember
walking down the street beside
Uncle Eddie's legs
taking a nap in Mama's lap
talking to the pigeons in the park
I remember
my fuzzy hat, my yellow cat
my potty pot
I remember a lot
but I wish I remembered
what I forgot

Grandma's Bones

Grandma grew up
in the nineteen-forties
she can still do the jitterbug
a dance they used to do
to the music of Duke Ellington,
Benny Carter, Count Basie
and such

she can spin a yo-yo
much better than I
and sometimes she puts
two sticks called bones
between the knuckles
of one hand and goes

clack clack clackety
clackety clack
clackety clackety clackety
clack clack
uh clackety clack
uh clackety clack
clack clack clackety
clackety clack!

My Daddy

my daddy sings the blues
he plays it on his old guitar
my daddy sings the blues
and he plays it on an old guitar
he plucks it on the strings
and he sings about the way things are

he sings baby, baby, baby
I love you till the day I die
he sings baby, baby, baby
I love you till the day I die
well I hope you love me back
cause you know I don't want to cry

he sings 'Thaniel, 'Thaniel, 'Thaniel
boy I love you deed I do
he sings 'Thaniel, 'Thaniel, 'Thaniel
boy I love you deed I do
well you're a mighty fine fella
and son I'm so proud of you

my daddy sings the blues
he plays it on his old guitar
yeah my daddy sings the blues
and he plays it on that old guitar
he ain't never been on TV
but to me he's a great big star

Aunt Lavinia

Aunt Lavinia is the one
we never see
she keeps her address
a mystery
she's waiting for the
right clothes and a
house she's proud of
I wish she understood
about love

Weights

I heard my grandma say
Ms. Lomax look like she got
the weight of the world
on her shoulders these days
I saw Ms. Lomax sitting
at her window, and I think
it must be easier
to lift big barbells
than to lift weights
from shoulders

Who the Best

People always fussing about
Who the best
Who the best
This drummer or that one
This singer or that one
Making a big fuss about nothing
I say
What's the use of choosing
When we got 'em all
Anyway?

A Mighty Fine Fella

I don't want to be
Mr. Big
with a hundred different suits
counting my money in public
and showing off
in my new sports car
I'm a mighty fine fella
and I don't need things
to prove it

my serious man face
thinking
my laughing man face
my big Nathaniel me
moving through the world
doing good and unusual
things

I See My Future

I see my future
clear as I don't know what
not all the things around me
not furniture or houses
or sidewalks and stuff
I just see me

Watching the World Go By

sitting on my front steps
watching the world go by
I'm sitting on my front steps
watching the world go by
when I see all the trouble
I know life ain't no piece of pie

looking from my front steps
I can see the world go by
I'm looking from my front steps
seeing how the world goes by
when I see so much joy
I know I got to try

Nathaniel's Rap (Reprise)

Well, it's Nathaniel talking
and Nathaniel's me
Been talking about
My philosophy
Been rapping all day
Had a lot to say
Had to run it on down
Nathaniel's way
Okay!
It's time to rest now
It's time to go
I'm all rapped out
I can't rap no mo'
I got to go, hey!
Take it slow, hey!
Got to go, hey!
Good-bye!

A Note to my Friends

"Grandma's Bones" tells about some of the activities people enjoyed when I was a teenager in the nineteen-forties. Some of the boys I knew played the instrument called "bones," just the way Nathaniel's grandma does, moving their shoulders and heads to the rhythm as they played. Our ancestors had played this instrument in Africa, often using the bones of animals.

"My Daddy" and "Watching the World Go By" are written like the lyrics (words) of a type of music that's called "twelve-bar blues." Each verse is made up of three statements (they can also be questions). The first two are alike. The third is different but still related to the other two and rhymes with them. Each one is four bars long, making a total of twelve bars.

I think you would enjoy writing a twelve-bar blues poem. Turn the page and you'll find out how to count the bars.

Have fun!

Eloise Greenfield

A bar is a vertical line that separates notes in written music. Bars help you count the beats. The word "bar" is also used to mean the whole group of notes that appear between two vertical lines. In the verse below, there are four beats to each bar and twelve bars all together. Read the verse aloud. Pat your foot on each beat, that is, whenever you reach a number. You'll feel the rhythm.

```
my  |  dad - dy    sings    the    blues
       1            2               3

he  |  plays   it    on    his    old    gui - | tar                    |
4   |  1              2            3      4    | 1  2  3  4  |  1  2  3  4

my  |  dad - dy    sings    the    blues
       1            2               3

and |  he    plays    it    on    an    old    gui - | tar                    |
4   |         1              2          3      4    | 1  2  3  4  |  1  2  3  4

he  |  plucks   it    on    the    strings
       1               2           3

and |  he    sings    a - bout    the    way    things  | are          |               |
4   |         1              2            3      4       | 1  2  3  4  |  1  2  3  4  |
```